Beesto

on old picture postcar

CW01512300

Graham Hop

3. A 1920s view of a busy Chilwell Road, showing a nice line in fashion and the modes of transport of the day. To the right foreground is the road to Ellis Grove, and to the left, the shops on the corner of Imperial Road. The postcard was published by Nottingham firm C. & A.G. Lewis.

Contact us on 0115 937 4079 for a complete list of books published by Reflections of a Bygone Age
www.postcardcollecting.co.uk

Designed and published by Reflections of a Bygone Age, Keyworth, Nottingham 2015

Printed by
Adlard Print and Typesetting Services,
Ruddington, Notts.

Introduction

The Edwardian era saw the picture postcard become the most popular form of communicating news or messages, doing the job that phones and email do today. The picture side of the cards is an added bonus for collectors today, as illustrations covered a whole variety of subject matter. It was estimated that, by 1906, the British Post Office was handling over 2,000,000 postcards a day, 7 days a week and 52 weeks a year. However, the postcards were not just bought and sent for the messages: many were saved. *"Another card for your collection"* was a fairly common note added to the reverse of the cards. Families often had their own postcard albums, with embossed covers and dark grey pages, where the latest acquisitions could be slotted in. The popularity of the hobby continued after World War 1, but by the mid-twenties had virtually disappeared. The hobby lay dormant until the early 1960s, when those old albums and bundles of postcards came down from the attics and the tops of wardrobes, and began to appear in flea markets, jumble sales and antique shops. Today, postcard collecting is one of the most popular collecting hobbies in the U.K. today. There are specialist fairs and auctions held throughout the year and over fifty postcard clubs exist in this country alone.

Beeston is my home town, and forms the bulk of my collection of topographical postcards. Like many Edwardian towns, the 'social' life revolved around the churches and a thriving high street and shopping area. In addition, Beeston was on the main route between Nottingham and Derby, and beyond. There was also the Midland Railway line, the Canal and the River Trent, all attracting industry, workers and visitors to the area. Leisure time could be spent on the Recreation Ground, Dovecote Lane, or boating on the River Trent. There were also the public houses, and later, the Palace and Palladium Picture Houses. Major firms, such as W.H.Smith and C. & A.G. Lewis, and local shops, such as A. Paling, and Z. McKeand of Post Office Square were among many that produced postcard views of the town.

All the cards illustrated here were acquired after my previous book was published in 1990. As before, there are some great views of the leisure, shopping and business facilities. However, on this occasion I have also included rarer cards that portray some of the more residential areas. The majority of the cards are pre 1930, but I have added a few later views for your interest. This is not intended to be anything other than an illustration of how Beeston looked in times past.

Acknowledgement: I'd like to thank Grenville Chamberlain for the loan of three of the rarer postcards.

Graham Hopcroft
November 2015

Front cover: Although this postcard is captioned 'Nottingham Road' Beeston, it is believed to be a view of Broadgate as seen from the Nottingham University end. Tottle Brook flows under the road on its way to Highfields. The card was published in the 'Clumber' series (no. 647), and posted to Cleethorpes in October 1910.
Back cover (top): A much later multi-view postcard published by Valentine & Sons of Dundee c.1960.. It shows the War Memorial, Square and Town Hall, The Square, Recreation Ground (Broadgate), with the re-sited monument, and High Road.
Back cover (bottom): 'The Last Car to Beeston'. A comic card designed by F. Macleod a century ago, predicting that a tram to Beeston run by Corporation Tramways might be popular! It has come to pass at last! Signs on the top include *'To stop the car get on the line'*, *'Don't spit on the conductor'* and *'Do not eat your ticket'*. Bizarrely, it was posted in New Zealand in December 1912.

High Rd., Chilwell, Beeston.

4. A wrongly-captioned 1960s view of Chilwell Road. To the right foreground are a butcher's shop on one corner and the row of shops of the Victoria Buildings on the other corner of Hall Croft. *"Having a lovely holiday with Pat. You can see the spire of the church in this picture"*, wrote Lil, who sent the card to Perth in July 1967.

5. The Wesleyan Church viewed from Collin Street in 1905. It was built in 1902 for a congregation of 750. The shop on the corner was owned by Greensmith the grocer. Card published for Z. McKeand, Stationer, Post Office Square, Beeston, by famous national postcard publishers Wrench of London.

Beeston.   The Wesleyan Church.

Z. McKeand, Stationer, Post Office Square, Beeston. The Wrench Series, No. 8311

6. A rare c.1906 postcard of Hall Croft, viewed from inside the Chilwell Road entrance. In the centre are three fashionable ladies with two children, and a baby in a pushchair. The row of houses to the left are on Chesnut Avenue.

Devonshire Avenue, Beeston. No. 603.

7. Close to the town centre we have this view of Devonshire Avenue on a card published by C. & A.G. Lewis and posted to Sheffield in 1922. Clifton Lodge can be seen on the left, and a motor car is driving down the centre of the road towards Chilwell Road. *"We have had a real good day today. Went out at 5.30 to market on the dray"*, wrote Connie.

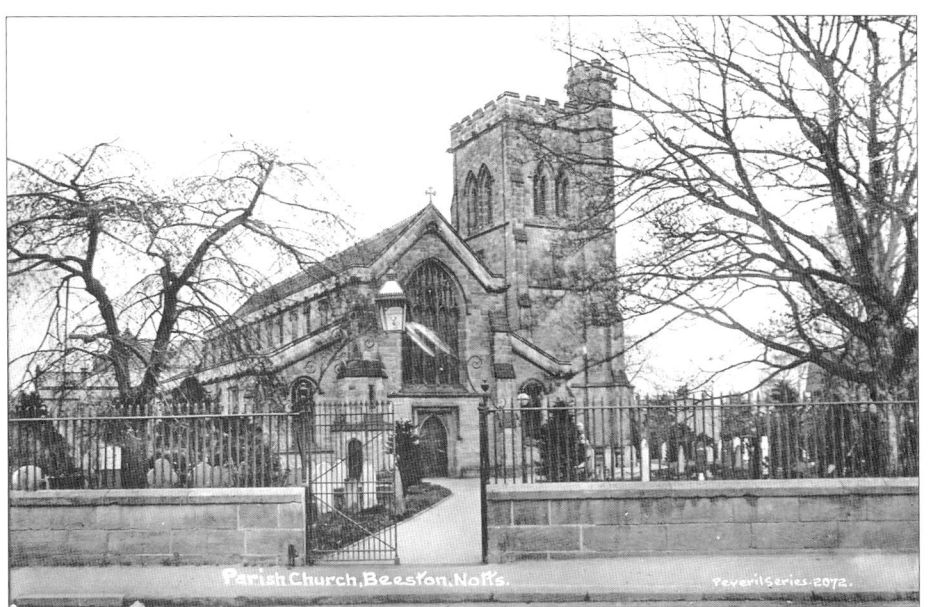

8. The Parish Church of St. John the Baptist, showing the walls, railings and the ornamental gates at the entrance to the church yard. Also on view are the gravestones, long before they were moved to the sides. In August 1913, Mother asks *" Are you getting plenty of bloaters to eat?"* of Arthur & Bethia, who were holidaying in Great Yarmouth. Postcard in the 'Peveril' series.

9. Superb view of the Square, as seen from the top of Church Street. The War Memorial is centre stage and the shops in the Commercial Buildings lead to the corner of Wollaton Road. The shop in the right foreground displays an advertisement for Cadbury's Chocolate. Postcard published in the 1920s by C. & A.G. Lewis.

10. Another view of the Square c.1960 published by A.W. Bourne of Leicester. Traffic lights are in place, though the only motor vehicle that can be seen is a van pulling out of Station Road. There are plenty of cyclists and pedestrians around. though. On the corner of Station Road, on the right, is the National Provincial Bank.

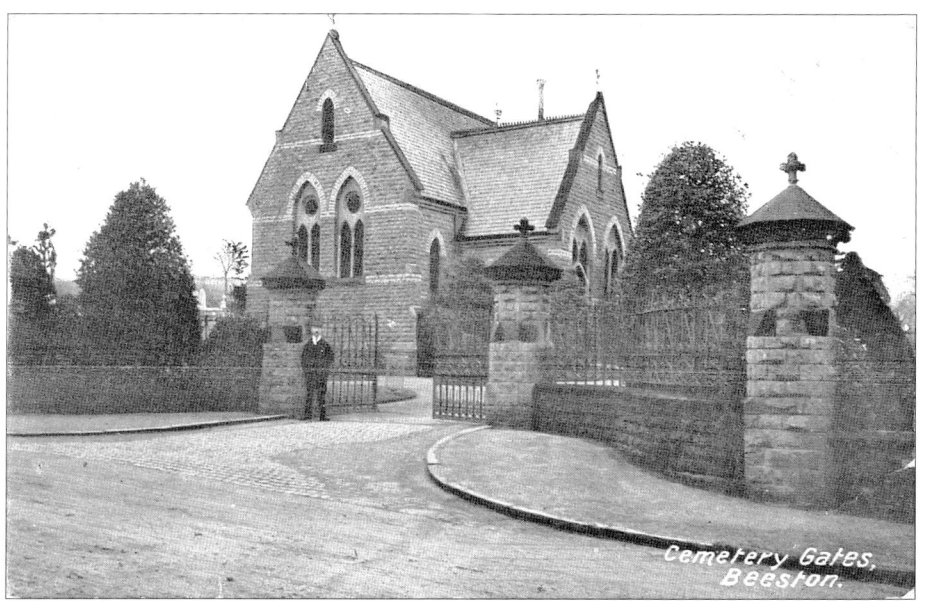

11. The Cemetery Gates, Beeston c.1905. These can be seen on Wollaton Road, on the way to the Derby Road. This card, not surprisingly, has not been postally used. Still, there is a good view of the Chapel, and the photo shows a chap standing at the gates.

12. New Beeston, Farfield Avenue, on a postcard in the 'Rex' series, no. 380 c.1930. This is the street where I was born, and where I lived for the first 23 years of my life, for most of the time in the first house shown on the left.

13. The 'new' houses on Wollaton Road. This card was published by Raphael Tuck & Sons Ltd. c.1950. The building of these houses began, so I believe, during World War Two, and the early ones were completed between 1942 and 1946.

14. Beeston Fire Brigade in front of their Station, located in Stoney Street. This is their new engine which went into service in January 1908. The engine, which was pulled by two horses, had a crew of twelve men, while the other three seen on this card were probably council officials. Card published by A. Paling of Beeston.

15. A scarce postcard of Cromwell Road, Beeston. The view shows the section from below Park Street, and the road off to the right is North Street. Posted in August 1929, the message begins, " *I thought you might like to have a local card - tried to get one of your road. This is the nearest approach*". Postcard publisher was John Henry Spree.

16. Another scarce postcard, also published by Spree. This one is of Enfield Street, Beeston c.1929. The view is from Hope Street and shows Cromwell Road crossing mid-distance.

17. West & Co.'s. Clothing Stores - 'For Mens Wear, or Boys Wear', c.1915. The shop stood on the corner of the High Road and Station Road, and was a men's outfitters for many years, once owned by Victor Oades.

High Road, Beeston. No. 602.

18. Another view of the High Road, on a card posted to Pickering in 1926. " *Am having a fine time here"*, wrote Laurie. The shops on the right include A. Wilson and Shepherds the grocers. On the left is the prominent frontage of the old 'Palace Picture House'. Another card by C. & A.G. Lewis, no. 602.

High Road, Beeston. _ No. 3656.

19. High Road, Beeston, in the late 1920s. The shop of Mr. Bostock can be seen centre right, and a garage sign is in the foreground. No motor vehicles are in the picture, but plenty of pedestrians and cyclists. Card published by C. & A.G. Lewis, no. 3656.

High Road Beeston.

20. A very busy High Road as it was in 1953, with plenty of motor vehicles and shoppers around. The only shop name visible is Roses Shoes, on the right, with five ladies looking at the window display. Jean Forster wrote to Rosemary on the Isle of Wight: " I live at Beeston, a small town near Nottingham, I am nearly 13".

Humber Works . Beeston, Notts. 140.

21. The Humber Works featured on a postcard sent to Miss Betts of Leyton, London, in September 1907. " *... this view is of Humber Works. It is considerably larger than it looks, extending some distance to the left (where the arrow points). The room I am in is under the cross (top floor). I need some drawing material for a booklet for next month's motor show at the Olympia*".

Reading Room above
Bagatelle Room
Beeston Humber Institute. Dining Room
Music Room above
Humber Works in same Road this way ⟶

22. Beeston Humber Institute on another postcard sent to the same lady in December 1907. " *Am off to class tonight....*". Added to the front left of the card in pen are the descriptions '*Reading Room above, Bagatelle Room*' and '*Dining Room, Music Room above*'. Card published by A. Paling, Beeston.

23. Another scarce postcard. This one is of Marlborough Road, Beeston, viewed from the High Road, possibly in the 1940s. Not a lot to see on this card, but there are three adults and one child on the pavement (left) and a motor cyclist in the far distance. No publisher is credited on the card.

24. A great view of the High Road on this postcard published in the 'Rex' series in the 1920s. On the left is Waites, the newsagent's, and on the right 'The Greyhound Inn', whose publican at the time was Sidney Stone, 'The Durham Ox' and the 'Palladium Picture House' (or flea pit!). The postcard was sent to Shepherd's Bush in September 1925.

25. The High Road, looking towards the town centre, features on this postcard published in the 'Peveril' series, no. 3083, posted to Hampshire in September 1913. On the left is Greenlees & Sons (shoes) and, further down, a bank. On the right we see J. Bailey the butchers and Eastmans the grocery store.

26. Another High Road view, but closer to the town centre, where we see a ladies outfitters' next to Dorothy Nevett's shop. And there in the centre, next to Fred Hallams, is the wonderful frontage of the 'Palace Picture House'. Postcard published in the 'Rex' series, no. 398, and posted to Colne in July 1935.

Square & Monument, Beeston, Notts.

Beeston Monument.

A.P.B.
C.S.

27. The Square & Monument, Beeston, on a postcard published by E.G. White & Co. of Sussex Street, Nottingham. On the left, at the corner of Station Road, is the 'Nottingham Inn' public house and on the right the Star Stores. This card was posted in Sheffield in August 1906.

28. A closer view of the memorial for 'Hope', with the end of Chilwell Road in the background. The building to the left is the side of the Town Hall, in the Square. The postcard was published by A. Paling of Beeston c.1910.

Harold ✗ ✗✗ ✗ ✗ ✗ ✗ ✗

29. A closer view of the shops on the square in the commercial buildings that corner onto Wollaton Road. Most of the ladies, gentlemen and children appear to be posing for the photographer on the card, which was posted to Wakefield in June 1907.

30. This atmospheric postcard scene dates from around 1905 and shows Church Stre
hairdresser. Advertised on his window are Sherwood Rangers Cigars and Player's Navy
was sent to Newark in June 1905.

CHURCH STREET
BEESTON

ved from The Cross. On the left is The Beeston Toilet Saloon, owned by Mr. Morton,
rther up, on the left, we can see the 'Crown Inn'. The card, from an un-named publisher,

31. A real photographic postcard of the unveiling of the Beeston War Memorial cross, performed by Col. Sir Lancelot Rolleston KCB DSO of Watnall Hall on Saturday 21st May 1921. The architect of the memorial was Mr. William Herbert Higginbottem of Nottingham.

32. The Roman Catholic Church, which stood on Styring Street, is the subject of this postcard, published by C. & A.G. Lewis in the 1920s. A man of the cloth is standing by the church gate, and could the bungalow be his residence?

33. Beeston Lads Club, home of the 17th Nottingham Boys Brigade Company. The club moved to these purpose-built premises from the Anglo Scotia Mills in 1913. The message on this hand-delivered card to Sergt. D. Mee, reads *" Please attend the Club tonight at 7.15 for' C' Coy. Thanking you, J.R. Clayton"*.

34. Nether Street, viewed from Station Road, c.1914. The traditional cottages on the right and the house on the left have long gone, but there in the centre stand the grand buildings of the Nether Street Schools. Card published by Turner.

STATION R? BEESTON. (NOTTS.) 276-9.

35. A 1920s view of Station Road on this postcard published by The Doncaster Rotophoto Co. Ltd., no. 276-9. On the left we find Meakin's shop, which sold hats. Then we have F. Soloway next to F.A. Anela, decorator. Finally, in the centre, we see W.E. Groomes, a general machinist.

Beeston: Station Road   Rex Series: no. 365

36. An early 1920s postcard of Station Road, looking towards the town centre. We can see two ladies on the road and pavement on the right. On the left are three youngsters with brush, shovel and barrow, probably waiting for a horse to pass! A motor cyclist rides in the middle of the road towards us. 'Rex' series no. 365.

S 3193   THE CROSS, BEESTON

37. A view of The Cross, at the junctions of Grange Avenue, Dovecote Lane, Church Street and Middle Street. In the background is the Manor Lodge. *" This is a view quite near us, the way the ladies are going is one way home. I will point them out to you"* is the message. W.H. Smith-published 'Kingsway' series card, sent to Stockport in June 1916.

38. Dovecote Lane viewed from Queens Road, with the Recreation Ground on the left. There is a horse and dray centre left. *" Dear Miss Young, Many thanks for the parcel, Winnie was delighted, she will write to you, Wishing you happy Xmas"* wrote Mrs. Reid in April 1915, when she sent this postcard to Hoylake.

39. The John Clifford Baptist Church on Dovecote Lane. Sadly, the building was demolished in July and August 2015. *"This is the Union Chapel, your future religious home, kind regards"* is the message sent to A.E. Mellow in March 1905.

40. The Bandstand and Recreation Ground on Dovecote Lane. *'Dear May, Many thanks for your May letter which came to hand before I left... I am not stopping in camp as I have got a saddle room next to the horse. The master is staying in camp and I have a busy time with looking after the both of them"*, wrote Harry in May 1914.

AN AERIAL VIEW OF THE PHARMACEUTICAL FACTORIES OF BOOTS PURE DRUG CO. LTD. AT BEESTON, NOTTINGHAM.

41. An aerial view of the Pharmaceutical Factories of Boots Pure Drug Co. Ltd. This is a promotional card that states on the reverse that '*The buildings cover an area of 120 acres and provide employment for 4,000 of the 33,500 people employed by Boots Pure Drug Co. Ltd. and its retail subsidiary companies*'.

'AEROFILMS SERIES'   AIR VIEW OF THE BRITISH L.M. ERICSSON TELEPHONE WORKS, BEESTON, NOTTS.   NO. C 382

42. A view from the air of the British L.M. Ericsson Telephone Works, Beeston. Lars Magnus Ericsson bought the 20-acre site in 1903. It was built on modern lines and was self-sufficient, using rainwater and wood chippings in the boiler house. Card published by Aerofilms Ltd., Hendon.

Beeston Railway Station

43. Beeston Railway Station. From the bridge we see a train leaving for Nottingham on the left, and another on its way to Derby. Not only is there smoke coming out of the funnel, but steam is shooting out of the whistle. A super postcard published by R.W. Wharton, Post Office Square, Beeston.

44. The Station, Beeston. Notts. Timetables for the Midland Railway can be seen, along with adverts for Coombs, and AK Hole's ales. A group is standing by W.H. Smith newsagents. *" Burton won 13-0, Nottingham lost 21-5"*, wrote Chris in 1905, presumably referring to rugby union matches. The card was posted to East Stockwith vicarage.

45. Beeston, Clifton Bend. *" Dear Milly, Thanks for your P.C. Do you remember this view? I am really going to Canada on May 11th and have my ticket for the voyage Wish you were coming to Liverpool to see me off"*, wrote Hilda in April 1905. Card published by Wrench of London for Z. McKeand,. Post Office Square, Beeston.

46. Clifton Hall from Beeston. Lottie writes *"Dear Mabel. Thanks for P.Cards and pleased to hear you are having a good time. You are swanking motoring, that beats cycling. Well, dear, I hope you get this P.C. before you get back"*. The card, published by C. & A.G. Lewis, was sent to Blackpool in August 1916.

Clifton Hall from Beeston.

47. Lock and Pier, Beeston. This is a clearer view of the lock-keeper's cottage and landing stage. Two ladies in Edwardian dress can be seen on the towpath. Part of the message on the reverse of the card reads *"We had a guinea pig till last week when he died. We had him to keep the rats away"*.

LOCK AND PIER, BEESTON.

48. River Trent, Beeston on a 1920s postcard published by C. & A.G. Lewis of Nottingham. *"My dear Benny. Ask Aunty Mabel if she remembers falling in the Trent, & what a sensation she caused, love Aunty Lucy"*, is the comment on the reverse.

MITCHELL'S BOATHOUSE, BEESTON. B.W. SERIES. 108.

49. Mitchell's Boathouse, Beeston. Born in 1858, George Henry Mitchell started his boat business around 1888, hiring out rowing boats. He also had a pleasure steamer on which he ran trips to Barton Ferry, some two miles away. He passed away in 1945, aged 87. This is another Lewis-published postcard.

50. Nether Street Schools. Three ladies, a child and a baby in a pram can be seen on the right. The card was posted to a Miss Draper of Dursley, Gloucestershire, on June 28th 1914 (the fateful day when Archduke Franz Ferdinand was assassinated in Sarajevo and events set in motion that led to the start of the First World War) and reads *" Thanks very much for letter. Shall be home 6.30 on Wed. Are you going to Bournemouth next Sat. No, we shall not be going to Weston now. Hope to see you again soon"*. Card published by A. & G. Taylor of London.

51. A multi-view postcard, published by W.H. Smith, in their 'Kingsway Real Photo Series', and posted in June 1916 to an address in Stockport. It shows the Square & Monument, River Trent & house boats, High Road, Recreation Ground (Dovecote Lane), and the weir.

52. An unusual correspondence postcard from the Beeston Cycle Company. It shows the then Beeston standard of a bee on top of a ton weight. Posted in January 1922, the message reads, " *Referring to your PC of the 28th we are going into the question of Tricycles and will write you in the course of a few days*".

53. High Road as seen in the late fifties on this postcard published by Valentine of Dundee. The shops on the right include Dewhurst, Timpson's and Woolworth's. On the left are Fred Hallam's and 'The Palace' with its modern facade.

54. A real photo postcard of the Victory decorations as displayed on a house on Ashfield Avenue in the Beeston Rylands.

55. A 1960s view of the Trent Side, Beeston, on this card published by A.W. Bourne of Leicester. In the distance the lock-keeper's cottage can be seen. "*Do you remember this? It's a good view, so thought you would like it*" is the message on the reverse.

QUEENS ROAD, BEESTON, MARCH 20TH. 1947

56. The Beeston Floods of 1947. This view is of Queens Road on March 20th. In the centre is the Methodist Church, and to the right the sign for Beeston Boilers can be seen. The north of the High Road was barely affected, but hardest hit was the Beeston Rylands area.

HUMBER ROAD, BEESTON, MARCH 20TH. 1947

57. Another view of the Beeston floods of 1947, published by an un-named local photographer. This one is of Humber Road, and part of the Humber Works is on the left of centre, where the truck is.

58. 'Rex' series postcard, no. 371, showing the town's war memorial in the late 1920s.

59. A 'Greetings from Beeston' postcard published by A. & G. Taylor in their 'Reality' series, billed as a 'Genuine Silver Print Photograph'. The message, sent to Miss Tivey of Hyson Green in July 1908, reads *" The length of the skirt is 36 inches, waist 24 inches. Fanny will come tomorrow night?"*

A selection of other volumes in the 'Yesterday's Nottinghamshire' series (all A5 format with 40 pages):

'Yesterday's Nottinghamshire'
2. West Bridgford
4. Nottinghamshire Cricketers
5. Beeston
6. Nottinghamshire Railway Stations
8. Regiments of Nottinghamshire
9. Nottinghamshire Trams
10. River Trent
11. Retford
12. Cigarette Cards of Nottinghamshire
16. Newark
17. Nottingham's Lost Landmarks
27. Wollaton
31. Nottinghamshire Inns & Pubs Vol 2
34. Stapleford
37. Boots the Chemists
39. Nottinghamshire Collieries
40. Nottingham City Centre
42. Nottinghamshire Steam Railways in the 1960s
43. Nottingham Forest Football Club
44. Notts County Football Club
45. Nottinghamshire Post Offices
46. Goose Fair
47. Nottingham Castle
49. Robin Hood
50. Nottingham Events & Disasters
51. Nottinghamshire Steam Railways in 1960s vol. 2

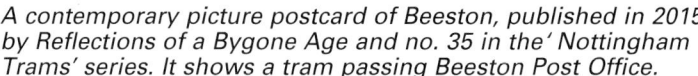

Nottingham tram and Post Office, Beeston

A contemporary picture postcard of Beeston, published in 2015 by Reflections of a Bygone Age and no. 35 in the' Nottingham Trams' series. It shows a tram passing Beeston Post Office.